DONKEY CHRONICLES

The Musings of Akiroro
Volume 1

Ebi I. Komonibo

KODGETI
PUBLISHING

Copyright © 2020 Ebi Komonibo

Kodgeti Publishing
All rights reserved.

ISBN: 9798568055129

I dedicate this book to my lovely wife, Mina.
Thank you for always believing in me.

i

Contents

A Donkey's Burden 2

The Human Dilemma 4

Bending Corners 8

As A Man Thinketh 10

Autoimmunity 18

Befriending Your Neighbor 24

Communication is Not Mud Wrestling 26

Corridors of Influence 30

Dreaded Bending Corners 34

Granny's Three-Legged Pot 40

How Many Enemies Do You Have? 46

Kaleidoscope in Humanity 52

Kiripoi – The Lost Art of Keeping Ears to the Ground
.... 56

Moving the Goal Post 62

Ownership Is in the DNA 68

Passive Persuasion 72

Patience 78

Periodic Table of Friendship 82

Discussion Questions 90

Glossary 98

A Donkey's Burden

Donkeys do not speak. They are beasts of burden who only shed real tears when the load gets too heavy. The only time a person recorded that a donkey spoke happened in the Bible. Balaam the misbehaving prophet heard the donkey talk, and then he mindlessly carried on an unfair discussion to blame the poor donkey.

When I dwelt on this sobering thought, it burdened my heart with heavy words and moved me to cry out. Once and for all, those who fear God need to ponder and decide where we stand and proclaim our truth, and this declaration of truth must foretell pertinent actions that encapsulate the motive which mere words may not be sufficient to uncover to those ignorant of our truth.

In *Akiroro's Donkey Chronicles*, I slip into the role of the donkey in the story through a series of soliloquies which allow you to eavesdrop on the donkey's conversations with himself. They require deep introspection for application. I write on what I see in these turbulent times, where many are lovers of themselves and the truth stays buried because people want their ears tickled by lies.

I am a Christian Izon man and my only allegiance is to the King of kings, not to any organization or group. It is the Lord God Almighty who gave me the voice to say what I believe He wants me to speak. I gain nothing by disrespecting anybody or massaging any egos, but I am thankful for the opportunity to share what I hear. If anything I say feels out of place, I assure you that my motive is clear: I most desire to reach those who are disposed to listen. To those who have ears to hear, God reveals all things in His time. Those who trust His sovereignty will not try to help Him. God is God, so we must let Him be God.

The Human Dilemma

The words of Akiroro, the donkey who talks to himself:

This world is full of trouble and you were born into so much trouble. Many issues vex your soul, but which one of you knows the timeless sure-fire antidote to this malady that plagues us all?

Why is it that you sometimes long to be on your own, but once you're alone you feel lonely?

You decide to change, yet the crowd overwhelms.

You lay low and feel depressed.

You choose to rise up, but your head feels dizzy.

You shield yourself and feel the discomfort of a hermit.

You give an embrace yet receive porcupine spikes instead.

You close your eyes and the darkness overpowers.

You look inside, only to see beyond your capacity.

You run, but have nowhere to hide.

You stay and the heat becomes unbearable.

You speak without sound; your voice has taken leave.

You refrain and the torrent within builds up like bellows.

You cry, but there are no tears to shed.

You laugh, but there is no joy in it; just an echo.

You smile, at least you thought you did, instead it was a frown.

You rest, but there is no respite in your constant tossing.

You eat, but the flavor has gone, leaving only a bitter aftertaste.

You swallow but your throat feels like you ate a cactus.

You wave goodbye, only to reappear on the same spot.

You wish you were dead, only to find it was a dream.

You thought you arrived, only to discover you haven't begun the journey.

You feel you are on top and look around to see you are at the bottom of the totem pole.

You think there is nothing else to know, but soon you find out that you know nothing.

You perceive that everyone else is wrong, yet you are driving the wrong way.

You grasp what you thought was everything, and then you realize you have retained nothing.

You out-scheme yourself from what you hold most dear.

You bear a grudge and end up mostly hurting yourself.

This is why you keep gathering your blessings in a pocket full of holes.

No matter how you run from reality, you will face dilemmas in life and there will always be decisions to make. The fate of any individual depends on making more right choices than wrong ones.

Bending Corners

When you were young, you thought about marriage and wondered how you would feel after finding the "one". But now, after many years, you no longer need to feel because you know.

Contrary to what you might think, the most important decision you make will concern who you marry and why you choose to marry them.

Trouble looms for the couple if the man marries a woman for her beauty, or a woman agrees to marry a man for material gain instead of what they may achieve together from the union. You find potential conflict or Bending Corners where blemish covers beauty and age does havoc on features; where fortunes take a hit and misadventures fetch the unexpected; when nature conspires to throw a curve ball and ill-timing from lack of planning inflicts surprises. When these conditions arise, panic attacks of the heart are bound to occur.

But despite your best efforts, it proved impossible to remove all the bending corners in your life. Just like on highways, the bends in life are inevitable to accommodate precious landmarks, by installing appropriate road signals to warn of a sudden approaching bend that might cause avoidable accidents.

As such, these bends can be envisaged and taken into account when deciding to engage or not to engage with other persons. And that is why full disclosure is important in any partnership, be it marriage, business or any association. Right from the beginning, it is best to bring everything out in the open because no secret stays hidden forever.

Self-disclosure is the most important step for anyone trying to engage another in a collaboration or partnership, and whatever you divulge should be an authentic expression of yourself and your motives. If what you disclosed obscures your motive, it carries the risk of a Bending Corner.

For any joint venture to be successful, the partners must form a habit of communicating truthfully. If both of you are not honest from the beginning, the steps of that relationship will most likely lead you into a ditch.

As A Man Thinketh

"As a man thinketh," the Bible tells us, "so is he."

As you think, Akiroro, so are you.

You are a product of your thoughts. Your environment, perception, and the activities you choose to do influence your thoughts. For this reason, your head will often lead your heart to where your head wants to go, even though you think you are following your heart.

In other words, your head and your heart are like an old married couple who drive everywhere together, and your heart is habitually the passenger who points out near misses and makes a lot of noise but really has no control over where the car is going.

Akiroro, why can't you understand that what you constantly think about is what you end up becoming or subconsciously try to emulate? That is why having a good head driving a healthy heart is important. Since it is a matter of choices amid many options, the good head must be willing to think and weigh all the possibilities. The good head knows that building a mansion in the slums drives down the value of a well-earned investment, but a bad head keeps investing money in the wrong places and risks being influenced by bad company because you are blinded by a singular goal.

At this point, you might feel the need to admit that you had a biased upbringing, which has saved you from many potentially difficult and embarrassing spots. Early in your life, did your father not teach you to stay away from situations where mudslinging and tempers run riot?

"If you do not avoid it," he warned, "you will be forced to learn the tricks of the trade in order to survive."

If it proves impossible to change the environment, you may have to adapt. Instead, adopt the "hear no evil, speak no evil, see no evil, think no evil, and do no evil" stance. Avoid evil and you will never miss it.

What happens when we constantly hear evil of someone or about a place, situation, or organization? Since we all naturally abhor evil, we build up our defenses and ready for imminent attack if we cannot get away. It is like the stirring of the hornet's nest. If the evil you have come to expect is true, that is well and good. But if that is not the case and what you heard has corrupted your mind, beware! You have bought lemons—

when all you have is sewer water—to make lemonade, hoping to quench that illegal thirst created by your inquisitive undisciplined mind. Contrary to popular belief, not every cloud of smoke signals a fire.

Listen, there is nothing as painful as running errands for an agenda that you are not party to because it is well-concealed. It hurts more to be caught holding the wrong end of the stick which you mistook for a baton. It is even worse if you are blessed with good memory and no good enough eraser to wipe evil from your mind. For such people, the evil stays and festers or propagates throughout its host and alters their signature character.

If you entertain evil long enough, it will dull the senses. Before you know what is happening, the unacceptable becomes permissible. That is how incitement works, slowly and seemingly innocuous on the surface. After all, the frog slowly heating in the bath never knew what killed it.

Speaking has a frame of reference, and you all copy what you hear others speak. Is that not how you learned languages? From a young age, you babble to imitate your parents and friends, copying how they speak. You judge what is good for your purpose, choosing and emulating the styles. In the same sense, if you stay around to listen to evil speak, depending on your choice, you either consciously learn or subconsciously imbibe the wickedness by growing accustomed to it.

Do you know how many alive today have tasted "*cabuluka*," a soap made from carbolic acid? If you haven't, just know it tastes disgusting. But if you are one of those adventurous types who likes to try everything, please go ahead and satisfy your appetite.

In some homes, *cabuluka* was the detergent for everything—including foul mouths. If you were caught speaking evil, your mouth was washed with *cabuluka* to stop the behavior in its tracks, because as an elder once explained: the evil in speaking evil is the possibility of spreading an otherwise localized non-issue which could have been contained or isolated.

Most times, evil speaking is selective, well-targeted and armed with a lethal weapon, like an artillery shell loaded with potent missiles intent on causing enough collateral damage to weaken or bring to total destruction. Often, evil is spoken in hopes that others will resonate with it, amplifying it enough to do the desired damage. If that is not the case, why would you choose to speak evil where there are good and better things begging to be said?

So when next you hear evil speech, pause to determine the motive and possible ramifications—that will quickly stop the itch. One of the questions you should ask yourself when offered some 'privileged' information is, "why am I so lucky to be in the know?" If you do not have the ready answer, you then ask how many others are special enough to know. Lastly, you wonder if you are being solicited as a courier. Are you going to be culpable for what others do with the evil information you do not need?

Some people are more affected by what they see than others. How many of you have regretted witnessing certain things? Like crazy glue on paper, some visions just stick, all day long, without warning or solicitation, terrible scenes of what you saw keep replaying at odd moments. Certain gruesome accidents are best not seen especially if you have photographic eye lenses and memory with automatic instant replay features. If you recently had such an experience and somebody says "Look," you might dig two of your fingers into your ears and use your remaining fingers to cover your eyes while you run away yelling "No," without a clue where you are going.

Never forget the power of suggestion in a simple look. If you look long enough into a deep pit, you may get dizzy, and if you stay long enough, you may fall into it. "Come and see the evil that so-and-so did," someone says, and you reply, "No, I don't want your generous offer."

If you know what is good for your life, you must not have anything to do with evil except to avoid it. Evil is distasteful and must not be tasted, lest you get acclimated to its bitter spices. When it comes to evil, be innocent but never ignorant of its devices. Looks can kill. If you attempt to look evil in the eye, it can kill you. Here lies the reason and purpose of the killer look, which most ignorantly glamorize. Shutting the eyes to avoid gazing on evil is a milder alternative to plucking them out to save yourself from getting into evil's ugly net.

At what point does a person begin to think? From the womb? Are there times when you truly believe that you can remember what you heard, what you spoke, what you thought about, in the days when you never understood what it meant to know these things?

The accumulation of these basic life events leads you into acting out the sequence of the things you do as influenced by those activities. If you listen too long to gossip, you learn to gossip. If you listen too long to messages of hate, before you know it, you are coining yours in droves. If you befriend someone with a violent temper, before you understand what happened, you will have learned the basics of Anger 101. If you are prone to speaking evil, before you realize it, you are buying your own lie—a consequence of a lie that had been packaged and sold to you by a companion of yours with a different motive.

If you choose to think evil, it will ultimately accumulate to become powerful enough to wreak havoc on other persons. Here, the principle of precipitation is useful to explain the dynamics of good and evil. It takes just one snowflake to start a snowball, so you should not ignore the "innocent" evil trying to gather in your mind. Expel it! If one act of evil is allowed, others will follow to build Fort Evil. What you hear, what you speak, what you see, what you think and what you do are all embodiments of what you really are.

The words you say in anger often stem from previous thoughts. It is just that the controls to the relief valves momentarily got hijacked and malfunctioned to release what was in your subconscious mind. What the local drunk at the neighborhood bar said to you may not be accurate, but you can be sure that was not the first time he thought about it.

Thus, the Bible holds true. "The heart of man is continually evil", the weeping prophet wrote. Even after spiritual regeneration, hearing no evil, speaking no evil, seeing no evil, and thinking no evil are essential components of a lifestyle that inhibits doing evil.

As a man thinks, so is he.

The things you think about make you who you are.

Autoimmunity

If you continue to live despite the nagging feeling that everybody wants you dead, it is a clear indication that—besides youbody—Somebody wants you alive to fulfill your purpose. Whatever the cause of your perpetual loneliness and self-loathing, it is pertinent to understand that Somebody was careful enough to ensure that you are protected from even youbody amidst otherbody's perceived murderous intentions.

If you are sincere, you will admit you do not really know how and why you came into the world. Through the lesson of the birds and the bees told to you during childhood, your observation of the animals around you and the stories you heard from others, you may have been able to piece together and surmise early in your life how your parents contributed to your arrival in this place where you feel unwanted and hunted (at least in your mind).

The first protection you received as part of the gift of life was autoimmunity, where your body readily goes into self-preservation mode against any change or threat that affects your being. At birth, when you stopped receiving nutrients through your umbilical cord and sensed the coziness of the womb gone, you cried out in panic and that triggered you to take your first breath. In infancy, when you were hungry or in discomfort, you instinctively cried to signal your distress and were attended to. Those cries would be useful later in life, strengthening your lungs for activities such as singing and swimming underwater.

If like me, you were not a classically cute baby, someone must have taken the time to build your sense of self-worth. Children cannot be ugly in the eyes of their mothers and her love is part of the external autoimmune system that is inculcated early in the child's development. You grew up learning to accept and love yourself, and with time, how to respect and care for others despite your differences. Sometimes, things go wrong in this crucial development process and unintentionally, a guardian may be classified as negligent, dropping the ball, showing the first signs of trouble without necessarily being a hitman. Even in cases of negligence, someone must have taken the time to provide the nurturing that might have been overshadowed by those heightened insecurities.

Selective amnesia blots out the goodwill of others, quickly developing into a "nobody knows the trouble I've seen" mindset which precedes a nagging thought that everybody wants you dead. The mind is a powerful thing. If you hold on to an idea long enough and look for ways to justify it, it is possible to create that picture. The mind gathers missing bits and pieces to fill the holes, conjuring something that does not exist in reality. Until this external picture is complete, whatever captures the mind remains an undeveloped negative, formless and lacking its true colors.

If you base your value on the scars stemming from the negligence of a past that caused you to feel unwanted and unworthy, you are pushing the envelope of falsity and absurdity too far. The hitman of your imagination is a person like you, fighting to stay alive through their own litany of problems. The strong will to live in the midst of adversity is a key element of autoimmunity, which everyone is given right from birth as an inalienable gift.

Even if you look at your "unfortunate and ugly" reflection in the mirror and torment yourself with comparisons to the "fortunate" neighbor who reminds you daily of your subsistence, you may not totally like what you see, but that does not mean you will want to kill yourself. If you look in the mirror and observe the world around you, you will discover that your reality is actually dependent on the shared space occupied by you and your random targets of reference.

All the same, the story is quite different if this system is compromised, and the careless may compromise this gift by surrendering it to others. If indeed there are disparities within a common space, those who are different are not enemies but cohabiters who deserve to have their place in the community. Ordinarily programmed into you, the will to live is energized by self-love and propels you to thrive in spite of the difficulties that come with being different.

If you think further, those who love themselves enough will understand the freedom in the gift of life. To enjoy this freedom in the gift of life, you must know the Giver of Life because only the Giver knows the total value of the gift and how best to enjoy the gift. Sadly, many go through life feeling worthless and undeserving. They personally experience and inflict mindless pain to those they hold dear, having bought into the big fat lie that no one cares for them. Nothing could be farther from the truth.

God is the Giver of life and has a purpose for

every life He created. The fact that you are alive today is because the autoimmunity that He carefully programmed in you is working to ensure that you do not end your life despite the challenges you encounter. That makes at least two of you against the world—you and your Creator.

So the question remains: if God is on my side, why did He create individuals who could very well end my life if you gave into the lie that no one cares about you? Is it possible that the picture is blurry because your scars are distorting your vision? If an internal scar affects an optic nerve, you may perceive a person's open arms as raised fists.

If you follow the example of eaglets and chicks that eat what comes out of their parents' mouths, you shall likewise live and grow strong for purpose when you heed the instruction from above. Instead of entertaining fear, sum up courage and speak aloud that truth which comes from God, scriptures you consumed in the past such as "I shall not die but live and give glory to God" (Psalm 118:17).

The Word of God is the premier autoimmunity system of life for those who have received immunity through faith in Jesus Christ. As part of the "live and let live" diet, the Creator has this important menu: "Man shall not live by bread alone but by every word that proceeds out of the mouth of God" (Matthew 4:4).

These words are life, and those who frequently visit this heavenly restaurant to dine on this divine menu will discover a whole new meaning to life, fueled by a recreated past that launches them into a glorious future.

Befriending Your Neighbor

Friendship cannot be legislated, just as peace cannot be mandated. Ill feelings, which often develop between two individuals, can spread to families, communities, tribes, and nations if left unchecked. The only way to recover trust—a key ingredient in developing and maintaining friendship, and by extension good neighborliness—is to start to be engaged one-on-one.

The Izon people make up the largest tribe in the Niger Delta. There is a price to pay for being large. If the Izons are to take leadership in the call for justice for the Niger Delta because of their size, then hearts must be large enough to recognize the opposing views from minority groups and try to win their confidence. It will be undoubtedly difficult, but with the will to do unto your neighbor as you would have him do unto you, it can be done. The world is a small place and oppressed people cannot afford to fight themselves forever.

History has taught that lesson; Izon communities who were under the old eastern region will understand. In the not-so-distant past, "minorities" like the Izons were once the Achilles heels.

With that in mind, these obstacles must be managed. Consider how frightening it is to be a minority when distrust and fear are two formidable tag team partners in division. But you can separate these two by tackling individuals one-on-one, creating friendships across communities who can then influence and allow their goodwill to be understood amongst their circles of influence.

"Them vs. us" tactics are counterproductive in any team, and a good leader must find ways to eliminate them. Keep pressing on, Izon!

Communication Is Not Mud Wrestling

If you were in your Sunday best and an aggrieved counterpart who was doing his daily business in a mud pit challenged you to a match, what would be your response? If you turn down the offer and just as you turn away, your determined opponent flings some mud on you as a last resort to change your mind, what would you do?

What is more tolerable, to become a victim of mudslinging or to dive in the mud bath and duke it out? Mud wrestling has no winner—it simply determines who is wise and who is not. Though both participants are covered in mud, it is the one with the wrong attire who will be the butt of the joke for his foolishness.

It is wise to trust your family and friends who tell you the truth all the time. Because you value them, you take some of the selective stories they tell you at face value. Trusting but not gullible, it is your hobby to listen in on discussions—you consider interesting—held aloud in public. One time, you heard this interesting story about two friends who had a private misunderstanding and one of them went on the internet and totally lambasted his opponent. The betrayal resulted in an all-out battle, a referee-less free-for-all with as many cheerleaders and mercenaries each side could muster.

In your silly thinking, you wondered why things escalated, and this thought was immediately met with the answer: This is why, silly. A fight for supremacy is meaningless without an audience. If it is just a question of misunderstanding, the two can quietly resolve it in private, often without further words. With just a simple gesture (a nod, an embrace, a handshake), the matter is a done deal and everyone goes their merry way. But if the conflict is more about a power struggle, there must be an audience to identify the winner screaming "Who is your daddy?" while the loser bears the mat marks as reminder of who is superior.

Before you laugh, think back to the last time you boasted about what you did to someone for crossing you. Were you simply telling a story, or were you seeking support that you did not need for a "battle" that was a mere disagreement? And did it help relieve your anger, or did it only fan the flame of your offense?

In this technologically tense world where apps are being cranked out faster every hour of every day, there is a tendency to overlook the importance of having a heart-to-heart discussion and resolving issues one-on-one. In a typical tech-savvy family these days, members no longer talk but text even when in the same room. With each face glued to your respective mini screens, the valuable lessons you can learn from reading facial expressions are lost as you type and tap away. How are you going to avert potential trouble in proximity if you ignore the clenched fist or funny expression of an offended sibling? A good look into your counterpart's face to check their demeanor may instantly give you the signal that it is not a good time or the message you are sending is not well-received. As such, you either repackage and reroute or stop!

(This is not a handout for the mud wrestler but something to consider if you are not interested in dirt.)

Corridors of Influence

Egberi ama binyien gali yama — "stories with protruding backsides."

Akiroro, do you remember the first time you heard this expression? It was in a conversation between your late mother and her sister. Decades later, you still remember being confused as a five-year-old as to what your favorite auntie meant. As you grew older, you came to understand this was her standard expression for any story that was hard to believe. Your auntie was a straight shooter (a fierce one), while your mother was the more diplomatic of the two. Your mother was the calming balm whom your auntie adored and respected. For your auntie, any story that was not straightforward had a protruding backside which must be inspected for authenticity.

Early on, your siblings and cousins learned not to tell any cock-and-bull stories around your auntie because they knew she would put such tales through fire to test them before taking you at your word. You never told unsubstantiated stories, or bring home bad reports, and you certainly did not bear information that contained

"They say." If you could not confirm the source, you knew not to tell the story within her earshot. Since childhood, you have carried this same affinity for verified truths.

Another influence this graceful woman had in your life was her undying love for her older sister. As an inquisitive homebody child, you were fascinated by the way they related with each other. Despite being separated after marrying husbands from adjacent towns, the two sisters spent their lives working closely together on farms. In your childhood, you never observed a cross word between them. By her example, your auntie taught you to love and adore your older brother just as she did her sister.

At a young age, you learned to tell it as you saw it—which often spells trouble for children, unlike your brother, who was and still is in the business of sharing only what is important. He had only one bone to pick with you, since you were in the habit of volunteering information, both his personal business (which he preferred kept) as well as your joint business (which you did not mind sharing with details). This point of contention was most swiftly dealt with away from your parents, so as to create respect and authority. The pull of his love was always stronger than any pain— and there was pain— but you would have never known it by how you stuck to his side like his shadow. You love and adore your big brother, and the funny thing is he loves you more.

Now, as a parent and an uncle, you wonder what lessons your relationships with your siblings have taught your children. Have you influenced them the way your auntie of blessed memories influenced you?

What would happen if everyone took the time to love those around them, not just for what they could get from them but also to teach the young ones what love is all about.

You never know: your favorite expression today could become the mantra or guiding principle for someone who values your person, and that is a life of influence. A life of affluence is external, personal and limited, but a life of influence is internal, elastic and far-reaching.

Thank God for people like Auntie Grace, and anybody can be that role model for others. No individual has two heads. Being impactful may not be easy, but what matters is that you have tried your very best. Because your best might be all it takes to change the course of someone's life.

Dreaded Bending Corners

The other day, you caught yourself in a joke asking a Nigerian friend of yours who hadn't been home for years if he'd been waiting for you at his bending corner. While the meaning of the phrase was totally lost on your poor friend, your visiting relative burst out laughing and asked where you got the expression from.

Another equally baffling expression is the suggestion that someone "hug a transformer" when they have offended you. The prevalence of such expressions and their implications reveal a troubling social condition.

There was a time when if someone was offended or aggravated, their options would be to bite a pillow instead of spewing venom; punch a bag instead of punching the daylights out of someone; kick something hard and yell out in pain rather than doing bodily harm to the offender, or tell the offender to get off your case and take a hike; ask the seasoned swimmer to jump into the river and cool off because you know they will not drown. It takes two to tango. For a fire to be sustained, there must be fuel.

Most often, we are not fully aware of which is more dangerous: the fuel or the ignition. In the absence of either the fuel or the spark that sets it off, there can be no fire. But together, they make an explosive combination.

Defined simply as traps or snares, bending corners are inimical to every element that builds healthy interpersonal relationships. Those who resort to bending corners use their intellect to devise schemes that trap the unsuspecting and unassuming. Similarly, the thought of asking an offender to go hug a transformer is not only ridiculous but carries worrisome latent danger. Figure this plain statement: for offending my sensibilities, go kill yourself and live no more so you will not bother me or anyone else! It sounds callous when put bluntly and interpreted literally. Rather than asking the offender to leave the scene ("buzz off!" or "take a hike."), you are wishing the permanent exit of the person not only from your life, but from all lives, including that person's loved ones who know no better. (Such a capital punishment for daring to offend the one that believes they have offended none.)

Everyone talks of justice and everyone will one day need mercy, but few are willing to show grace to one another. No matter the frequency or the levity, the day you are denied what you need from someone with the resources to help is the day you wished everyone in the position to help would do so. There is a bend in every living being, and these have the capacity to offend those we come in contact with. If relationships are considered flowing streams, then bends form riptides that create turbulence in the flow. The tighter the bending corner, the more difficult it becomes to navigate a space. These difficulties slow down traffic and bring to a halt all hopes of a fruitful exchange. Your individual bends are troublesome in themselves, so intentionally setting up well-crafted bending corners to trip up the already-bent, in order to watch the inevitable fumble of the disabled is unbrotherly.

The voice has not left the people. But the discomfort that bending corners establish in social settings often silences you who have something to say, resulting in a noticeably unbalanced conversation. In these moments, you might lean towards self-preservation, choosing to remain "safely" on the sidelines to watch victims get clobbered as the bending corners tighten. Unfortunately, the euphoria of verbal sparring will eventually fade. Once you have run through your opponents, there will be no one left in the arena.

Lately, even your invisible dog "Sit-down Look" has been signaling you to be even more introspective on this matter. On a warm night, you watch the moon and wonder why there are bending corners in places where ideas are meant to flow freely. Where is grace when you need it most? What is the point of gathering to isolate ourselves from each other? Why the need to be tightfisted when you can afford to give others without cost? If you have not yet learned to give that which costs you nothing, how sure are you that you will suddenly know—without practicing—how to share among others, talk less of actually making a sacrifice? Giving the benefit of the doubt costs nothing, but one day, something about you will come into question, and you will wish that someone gave you the benefit in that situation. To secure this goodwill, you must pay it forward. There are no other ways around it. You either pay it now or risk being bankrupt on the day you need it!

And so you should consciously review your motives in relation to one another. Try to focus on what you can individually do to accommodate other people rather than creating self-defeating bending corners.

It is a free world, so be real to yourself and

consider your own wishes, prayers (if you are so inclined) and motives. Your authenticity will not be judged by the perception of the millions blinded by your flamboyance, but by the impact felt through your small and genuine efforts made over time.

Granny's Three-Legged Pot

The traditional three-legged pot is made of iron, but ironically it could break if handled carelessly because it is made of cast iron. In those days, options were few, so you might wonder why anybody would still bother to cook with a three-legged pot when there are now many reliable brands of pots. If your grandmother was alive today, she would explain why by giving you an earful about the wonders of the three-legged pot, enough to write a cookbook. But in her absence, you can only remind yourself of this wonderful contraption.

Although times are different, there are things that have changed and things that haven't. In Granny's days, families were exceptionally large and, no matter how large the families were, food was cooked in and served from one pot and those pots were huge!

Growing up, you particularly remember three-legged pots as tall as five feet, where an adult cook required a stepping stool to see what was cooking in the pot. These giant pots were mostly used to process palm oil and cook large meals to entertain guests during festivals and ceremonies.

In comparison, clay pots were mainly used by the poor and those who craved its distinct flavor. There was always the structural strength limitation to the size of the clay pot. On the other hand, the 55-gallon metal drum was used for processing palm oil, but it was not considered aesthetic or classified as a pot.

The three-legged pot is an effective heat transfer medium compared to other pots. While you would need to be careful not to apply the fire all over other pots, the three-legged pot fears no heat. If so desired, the whole pot can be engulfed in the inferno it is used to right from the molten state it was made. You hear of smoked beans, smoked that, the smoking is ingrained if desired. The loveliest thing about cooking with a three-legged pot is not only in the cooking and the great dishes it produces, but also the ease of maintenance. You cannot make charcoal any blacker and charcoal from the fireplace contain no germs (there are carbon filters and purifying edifices these days), so the outside of a three-legged pot needs no washing. Much to your delight as a kid doing chores, you'd simply wash the inside free of food particles and leave the outside carbon black. When a child volunteers to wash a pot, make sure to check it afterwards; it is either very easy to wash or there might be something left inside it (on purpose).

Big boys, you now know why you are forbidden to lick the bottom pot, since it will set in motion a delayed program that would spook your guests during your wedding by a heavy downpour, leaving no one in doubt what you did: you licked the bottom pot which was left for the girls who usually wash the utensils.

This exposé would not be complete without a most important observation that Granny would have wanted you to make. The three-legged pot has an unparalleled tenderizing effect! When you live in a severe terrain, you eat whatever is available and edible. The elephant is considered a tough meat. Among Izon people, if food takes a long time to cook, the hungry would ask the cook if it was the genitals of an elephant. The second runner up in the hard-to-cook is the manatee. In the West, this reclusive mammal is protected, but in the Niger Delta, the endangered species eats whatever is delicious and nutritious to survive on.

Manatee burger! Elephant steak! These meats would be frustrating to cook in conventional pots without the addition of potash or other meat tenderizers. Neither your Granny nor you know the science behind it, but the cooking time is reduced to at least half when nails or wrought iron are placed inside the conventional pot, or when a three-legged pot is used to cook tough meat. So the next time you cook your oil-less *okodo* (unripe plantain with goat meat) in a three-legged pot or in a conventional pot with two or three nails (make sure you take them out afterwards to be complete or your family gathering might turn into a whole another affair), remember Granny as you enjoy the unique taste.

The three-legged pot is not like other pots you have in your kitchen and you would not treat it like your other utensils. For one, the pot is ugly and could easily soil your garments if you decide to handle without caution. It may be too large to handle. Special care must be taken when removing it from the fireplace since the entire pot including the handle is hot. If another object is carelessly placed over the pot and that object falls upon it, the pot may break beyond use.

And so, you might now wonder why anyone would bother cooking with such a finicky pot when you can get by with other less cumbersome alternatives. The answer is simple: Taste! It is a matter of taste. A matter of economics, expedience and convenience. Some people like 'party rice' for the smoky taste and nothing does it better than the three-legged pot.

Granny's lesson from the three-legged pot is

simple: Work with what you have, understand its characteristics, improve on the positive and, if possible, mitigate the negative to live with the outcome. The three-legged pot can be broken only once, and when that happens it is useless. The disadvantages are mere restrictions which call for caution but do not make it useless unless someone goes against the known restrictions. Everything that has use or utility has certain restrictions which must be observed for the thing or relationship to remain functional. In several instances, the law of pick-and-choose may be limited.

Roses are beautiful and full of fragrance, but roses come with thorns. The total package includes both the pieces and packaging that preserves the pieces. Even in this age of constant makeovers, there are things best left alone. No matter how noble your intention, insisting on changing a friend is like applying spit polish to a situation. All that is left is an ashy mess and the spell of the spit.

Any long-term friendship has endured for at least one good reason, otherwise it would have ceased long ago. If you complain about your friend whom you consider slow and yet you always go to that friend for a second opinion, then you have acted rashly.

It follows that when you want to enjoy the fragrance of good things such as friendship, you must be willing to accept the total package.

How Many Enemies Do You Have?

If you must be responsible and keep good accounts of the things that are yours, then you must ask: how many enemies do you have?

In truth, you cannot know how many enemies there are. Though you may think you know some of them, even that is debatable! If you are unsure of who your true friends are, how can you tell how many enemies you may have, when there are those whose modus operandi is to hide under every imaginable charade and strike when least expected.

If staying alive is your goal, yet you cannot account for all your enemies—both real and imagined, how can your safety be guaranteed when it takes just one enemy who is stronger than you and determined to finish you?

And if your number one goal is to stay ahead of your enemy's antics, how can you be successful without first identifying your foes? Without careful thought, you begin playing blind man's bluff, slashing and striking objects that exist only in your head.

Now, take a moment to ransack your head because there is another question that begs an answer.

If you cannot count all your enemies, let alone identify all of them, how possible is it to guide yourself from being overpowered? How do you begin to create an antidote to a poison that no one can identify? How easily you can die or be taken prisoner, all because of your lack of knowledge. And yet, when it comes to identifying what is inimical to your wellbeing, you would deny your potential to be your own worst enemy.

You go on in life blaming everybody, especially those closest to you, and totally absolve yourself instead of acknowledging yourself as a potential enemy. Without thinking, you run the traffic red light of life and turn around to blame the camera that caught you red-handed. You fail to apply the brake but attempt to exonerate yourself by shifting the blame to the mechanic for a shoddy job.

Make no mistakes about the matter, there are many unseen enemies out there. So what are you going to do about it? One approach would be like some cosmic cowboy looking for enemies in every nook and cranny, vigilantly shooting at anything in sight, adopting the Canon camera slogan, "If it moves, shoot it with a Canon."

This mindset dictates that if any action is suspicious, shoot first and investigate later. In desperate situations, "act first, and if you are wrong, ask for forgiveness later."

The problem is that this habit of bouncing between offense and repentance can be abused. How many times can forgiveness be granted before the limits are exceeded? If you do not act wisely, you may find yourself in a world full of countless, faceless enemies whose offenses affect your psyche to the point of paranoia.

For every problem or dilemma there is a solution. Fortunately, this particular solution stares you in the face—it is found in the Word of God. But because you have grown familiar with the Bible, turning to it for answers has become counterintuitive to you.

The Bible tells you that the enemy's goal is to offend or hurt you, which is why the entity is called your foe. If you cannot account for all your enemies and their various activities, what is the prudent approach when you uncover an antic of an enemy? Your response will determine whether you are going to win or become a prisoner.

Here is the suitable Word for the situation:

[19]Do not take revenge, my dear friends, but leave room for God's wrath, for it is written: "It

is mine to avenge; I will repay," says the Lord. [20]On the contrary: "If your enemy is hungry, feed him; if he is thirsty, give him something to drink. In doing this, you will heap burning coals on his head." [21]Do not be overcome by evil, but overcome evil with good. - Romans 12:19-21 (NIV)

This message is simple but deep. When God says He will repay, it means He will undo what the enemy did to you and He will get even with the enemy for his actions.

If you choose to take it upon yourself to pay back evil for evil, what of those enemies that you as the paymaster do not know or cannot reach? Are you willing to become both the jailor and the prisoner, with the hidden key of forgiveness in your pocket?

The Bible says, "Make room"—meaning move out of God's way. When it's time for God's wrath to take out your enemies, He lines them up like a seasoned bowler knocks down pins lined up in an alley. So if you must do something, there are better things to do. Instead of counting "enemies" and their limitless offenses, everyone you identify or perceive as such should be treated better than they deserve or what you have received from them.

When you repay evil with good, one of two things is possible. Your perceived enemy might react positively and become a friend, or the offense can be neutralized because the misunderstanding that may have created the perception has been cleared.

On the other hand, if it is a real and determined enemy, you have cleared your conscience by demonstrating your goodwill and established your innocence to make room for God to be your defense. God is bigger than all your enemies combined and has promised to fight for you if you leave matters in His capable hands.

Your enemies will try, but they will not succeed—though that may not stop them from more attempts to hurt you. Some will keep pushing the innocent until they get taken blindfolded into the palaces of their avowed foes and force-fed with goodness that is alien to them, which can cause confusion and unbearable shame.

To that end, the good news is that the acquisition of a loyal friend out of the fiery furnace of a once avowed foe is priceless, far beyond the cost of the milk of compassion, or the cost of you turning the other cheek.

Kaleidoscope in Humanity

You see in colors, but you dream in black and white. If you gaze at bright colors for too long, you face the danger of being blinded. Yet when you dream long enough, you may get illumination from within. They told you that many colors constitute the rainbow, and the color white is a composite of all colors. To see in the dark, an ordinary human needs light. In other words, you must examine every part of the whole to see the complete truth of an entity.

Humanity has developed devices to facilitate comprehension of the natural world and each tool has a specific function. The telescope brings objects from afar to be scrutinized up close. The microscope exaggerates minuscule sizes for close inspection. The wide-angled lens captures things in view to establish timelines and relative positions. Every device has its place and the seasoned observer must select the proper tool for the purpose, or the result will be useless, no matter the cost or effort associated with the endeavor.

Just like gazing through an extremely narrow path culminates to tunnel vision, the undisciplined focus on a limited area causes blind spots that may lead to avoidable freak accidents.

When crystal ball gazing replaces the utilization of your mental faculties, it is a given that the reading will be out of whack, should the ball change colors randomly because the readings depend on the mood and bias of the reader.

It is perfectly okay to have a personal favorite color, but to insist on a color regardless of its suitability in the overall scheme of things is courting disaster. The choice of black clothing may be appropriate for an undertaker, but it would be ridiculous to mandate black attire for all those residing in a city that borders a desert. While color blindness may be an unfortunate natural aberration, excluding all colors beside what is pleasing or favorable is unwise. If the colors which are considered unimportant can no longer come into focus, that is mental blindness—the type of blindness others can see through but the victim cannot.

You do yourself a disservice when you hold on to your own views rather than borrowing the lenses of others with different perspectives. If you latch on to your own outlook without taking a bird's eye view of the issues at hand, how can you build to last or fit for purpose when you lack the required focus? How can you find something without knowing what you are searching for? And if you do stumble upon something, how can you be sure it is what you have been seeking? Therefore, to be able to identify the "it," one must know the components of the whole.

A solid grasp of the big picture requires you to be amenable (and yes, amiable) enough to borrow lenses from others so you can identify the full spectrum of colors beyond just your favorite color.

There is a difference between borrowing and owning. To borrow another's lenses is to lease their point of view, allowing you to see what other colors look like. If the lens works, you now have the opportunity to unlock a new understanding of the rainbow in its entirety. If the lenses are faulty, it is fair at this point to gracefully discard them at no loss since they were borrowed and not yours to begin with. You suffer no ridicule from trying what turned out to be useless. Contrast that to snubbing the only lenses that could have provided you a complete image—how foolish, thinking you know it all only to discover you are the one who missed out on the majesty of the full picture.

Do not let your attachment to your own perspective prevent you from gaining new understanding.

Kiripoi - The Lost Art of Keeping Ears to the Ground

Do you know the origin or the exact meaning of the phrase "keeping ears to the ground"?

This phase of keeping one's ears to the ground comes up in situations where a hurried or careless action without due consideration may fetch adverse consequences. Existing clues and the solutions may be bypassed or missed entirely if observation is reserved only for specialized audiences. The footsteps of approaching troops from afar may be heard faster by keeping one's ears to the ground than from the air. In order to listen and have the advance warning of those given to standing, you must learn not only to stoop, but to lie low to the ground and hear what secrets the ground is willing to divulge to your humbled ears. This is the art of keeping one's ears to the ground.

Imagine a giant prides himself on his impressive height and fails to acknowledge the strength of the earth beneath him that bears his massive weight. Or the giant disrespects the eons of years the earth has been in existence, and the numerous giants and dwarfs the earth has carried, supported and buried. This is pride courting disaster and such courtship is ill-fated. Pride never marries disaster because disaster kills pride at the altar. Everyone in a less than desired situation has one asset above the neck. A good head—the nerves commanding center—must be protected. On the war front, the vulnerable head is given a helmet for protection. During war, you keep your head down to listen and guard against would-be snipers. Your control center must be the last point of access.

So why is it necessary to lie low to listen or dial into what is in progress? If you do not know what is going on, you are lost. There is nothing as bad as being lost in your own environment or what should be your turf. It is as if you are paying rent to another for your own property and facing the continuous threat of eviction. You end up paying for ignoring acquirable knowledge (this is ignorance).

Pride is like a chameleon, a flamboyant dresser that suits to fit the purpose. You can expect to hear expressions like "I am not interested," "I am too busy for such and such," "It is not important," "It does not mean a thing," "It can wait," or "Let others concern themselves with such trivial matters". The end is predictable. Disaster kills stylish pride at the altar.

God the Creator is the God of order. The Bible's account of creation is systematic, as chaos was brought to order by God's Spoken Word. That which comes before is older than that which comes after, and this remains as the One Who brought it about desires. If you came into the world before your siblings, you have seen your world and your joint environment before them, and there may be something you have witnessed that you have not yet divulged to them simply because they are not ready to receive it. Even if it is just one tiny piece of information, it could be the ace which may make or break their collective existence or sense of wellbeing.

If you were to go to a new city, you would be out of your mind not to ask for directions or observe how the citizens of the place behave before you take to the streets as you would in your hometown. The expression "Johnny Just Come" is not complimentary, but is indicative of one who came from Neither Land and sticks out like a sore thumb. If you do not keep your ears to the ground and sleep with one eye open, you face the danger of your lack of knowledge or self-discipline, causing you to blab and give away your naiveté.

It is unwise to advertise your ignorance. The best posture in unfamiliar territory is to keep your ears on the ground and listen to what the ground may reveal.

God created the Earth and placed man among trees and animals. Man disobeyed and sin entered to cause havoc and chaos which created your adversity. And still, by your own carelessness and stubbornness, you continue to create difficult situations for yourself and others. Like a broken toy, you scatter your misdeeds all over the place. Only when you keep your ears to the ground will you know how the original plan was meant to be, and then you can proffer the correct solution to the problem that is begging for the right answer.

Due to technological advancement, mankind has destroyed much of what nature put in place to sustain it. The Bible says the herbs are for the healing of the nations. Pay attention to what the goat eats when you catch malaria. Because while you shiver with malaria, the, 'foolish' goat relishes in the bitter leaf which holds the key to your cure!

How do you discover the potent mushroom with the extensive benefits and avoid premature death by ignorant experimentation? Observe the goat, as it differentiates between a potion and a poison. That goat's ancestors were there before yours and it is no coincidence that the goat is domesticated.

The ground was made before trees and animals. The animals were already here on earth before man got here. Though you may look sophisticated and claim superiority over the animals in your reasoning, you must not underestimate their extreme instinct which is responsible for their survival in places where human beings cannot last for any considerable period.

If you consider adverse situations and tie that to the part instincts play in survival, you may find some glaring correlation. God created the herbs before the animals and the animals came before man. The latecomers must learn from those who have been there before.

Observe domestic animals. Before man arrived, these animals survived in the wild without help from man, like how the goat needs no help from man. The Izon people liken the goat—which should be your favorite animal—to someone who is not reasonable or behaved foolishly. But this description is a first-class misnomer. When it comes to survival instincts, this animal is a shrewd die-hard, known for chewing just the right herb to recover from any ailment. If you could somehow bottle up the goat's ability to thrive under adverse conditions, with suitable backing, training and finance, you would become the next giant in the pharmaceutical industry.

In the end, you cannot find what you are not looking for. Even if you see it, you may not know it is since what is not useful cannot be found. To find what is useful, you must observe what is nearby, since the solutions to your problems are not farfetched, but scattered around like the dismembered toy of an angry child. You must look for solutions by keeping your ears to the ground.

Moving the Goal Post

If you provoke a donkey, it just might speak to you. And what the donkey says might be something you do not like. How worrisome it is when you randomly switch your cultural beliefs off and on, as if your culture has no basis for the things it upholds.

Cultural beliefs are like subroutines or canned processes that society put in place, and these widely known beliefs are followed by all to guide, answer and cater for situations that may emerge. These subroutines exist so that you do not have to reinvent the wheel in judging the validity of every matter that may arise.

In Izon, the culture is not to tell a lie. It is also known that a married woman should not bathe nude in the streams or rivers. It is Izon culture not to steal, and you must respect your elders, and there are many other beliefs the Izon hold dear. When these cultural beliefs were formulated, they existed within the prevalent cultural context at that time. Back then, women never went to war or joined war canoes, just as the culture forbade twins from joining their fellow men in war. But currently, those previous conditions are no longer present and so we cannot apply those same cultural positions and traditions to situations today. Therefore, attempting to evoke a set of traditions not applicable to the situation on the ground is like attempting to move the goal post.

As a child, you always wondered what would make a father refuse to send his otherwise brilliant daughter to school. This practice of depriving women of an education is an outdated and unreasonable tradition that should not be mistaken for culture. Instead it is a sad reflection of the myopic view of a few elders. When your grandfather chose to ignore your mother's undeniable mathematical genius, it was at great cost to you and your siblings. You were denied the benefit of early learning and help with homework, among many things. To mistake idiosyncrasies as cultural norms would be the greatest mistake and enough provocation to move this donkey to speak.

In your society today, women have gone to school and demonstrated their natural advantage of multitasking over men. It can be quite humbling for men to learn that in certain things they are mental midgets compared to women. If not kept in perspective, these differences can be viewed as adversarial rather than complementary. Do you remember some encounters you had with female classmates and colleagues that serve as constant reminders never to dare think that women are inferior?

When a woman bravely performs duties that even some would not do, you cannot deny her strength in other settings by evoking irrelevant cultural norms. It goes that if you are ready to receive a shield in war time from a woman wearing a skirt, it is also right to receive leadership from her if she is proven to have a good head in addition to a good lion heart. But as anyone knows, you should be more careful approaching a lioness with cubs than a roaming lion, since you know the interest the lioness is protecting, and if you have some sense, you will avoid messing with her. Someone who preaches peace and unity in times of chaos should be given the opportunity to help realize the future that motivated and fueled the doggedness.

Izon culture clearly states that you should never remove ancient landmarks, and the corollary—which is also true—says that you must not plant landmarks in the middle of the fields, because doing so will bring confusion among neighbors. Hence, the ever-green tree *ogirizi* is reserved for groups and families to demarcate boundary lines. The tree must not be planted nor uprooted by single individuals. Even forest fires, whether natural or caused by mischief, cannot destroy this hardy tree.

In the same vein, it is illegal to move a goal post when the game has begun, or try to make up a rule during the game. Such rule changes are unjust and should not be tolerated. And yet the powerful often succeed in these illegal movements without opposition because most do not feel the pain of those who were on the verge of scoring a goal when the post was suddenly moved.

The basic feeling of empathy is lost to many in this age where the top dog eats all, while all others are viewed as stray dogs scrambling for the leftovers. And this scramble for the top dog position ignores other equally important roles like the watch dog, guard dog, seeing dog, fighting dog, smart dog, guide dog.

The excessive fixation with the top spot has turned the journey to be top dog into a fierce and callous debacle. Those who aspire to fill any position must be cultured and suited to fit the office, and the determination of the qualifications must be systematic and understood by everyone for each person to be placed in their proper roles.

Most of all, the rules of engagement must never be changed in mid-stream, since any mismatch will put the entire organization in jeopardy.

Ownership Is in the DNA

Hear ye all parents, whether you are abroad, outboard or onboard, it does not matter. The war is at your backyard, so do not fool yourself. There is no place to hide for you who make the choice to lay down and produce children and then renege parental responsibilities. There is equally no excuse for you who never bother to play an active role in raising the children around you to become responsible citizens. If you neglect children when you have the opportunity to influence them, you will regret the adults they grow into.

You cannot boast in the success of an individual if you did not play an active role in their development. For you absentee parents, though your only contribution to the achievement was your DNA, the attachment between parent and child is irrevocable. In the same vein, it would be improper to disown a child based on their behavior, whether right or wrong.

In Izon, "*Ebikaaki*" means it is mine only when it is good; which is an extremely dangerous approach of distancing oneself from what is unpleasant. Identifying and taking ownership of what is yours (both good and bad) enables you to deal with issues as they arise.

Sorry, but you cannot "hide under a stone". If you do, a boulder might roll over you and crush you underneath. You must be willing to collectively employ useful solutions to save your children and your communities from impending doom. It might be another person's family facing hardship today, but tomorrow your family could be next.

So what have you done with the family God gave you? Regardless of if you believe in God—which is another matter entirely—what has been your response to the threat of your children being influenced and subverted by forces you have no control of? No matter where you reside or sojourn, whether a homebody, nomad or living in the Diaspora, your children are in danger of being affected by their surroundings.

The home is the place to start building immunity from the conditions that make one prone to violence and revelry. You cannot afford to pass the buck or shirk the responsibility of parenthood while expecting payment as deputies who never did any work. Yes, for every work (including bringing children into the world), there is a payment in proportion to the responsibility and role that was played or evaded. You reap what you sow and funny enough, children are the product of seeds their parents planted. When a certain outcome is dependent on various factors, the wise or sane thing to do is to take care of what you can at the moment. That is why well-tended plants produce the right yield, while plants you abandon to the elements produce sparingly, if at all.

In this world gone wild, you cannot stop birds from flying over your head, but you can prevent them from building their nests on your head. The tender children under our custody need the nurture and early tutelage to equip them to decipher right from wrong, as well as the skill sets to navigate the murky waters of adulthood. You cannot work in UAC and get paid in UTC. If both mother and father are outside the home all day leaving the children to fend for themselves, the modern-day babysitters (tech gadgets) that you entrust them to will surely fill their heads with whatever is trending (which may not always be a good thing). You must stop pointing fingers at victims drowning like heavy yams without life jackets on, while you stand watching by the edge of a deep and fast running river.

Being parents is not a day's job (or a night's job), but a lifetime of commitment to the wellbeing and welfare of a special person. As an adult in your community, you should commit to the responsibility of raising all children well and consequently saving those other children whose paths your own children might cross.

It takes changing one child—one family at a time to change society.

The ball is in your court.

Passive Persuasion

"If you make *gragra*, I make *krinn*."

This was a favorite saying of your high school biology teacher. A strict disciplinarian, the man was prone to meet opposition or any semblance of resistance to his authority head-on with greater force (but short of physical force). *Gragra* is not unusual for the average Izon man and your teacher was no exception.

So what exactly is *gragra*? It is...wait...*gragra* is when...you see, *gragra* is one of those words you clearly understand in your mind but to explain it in other words—especially to someone with no knowledge of the word—proves a daunting task. But if you were to try, you might say that *gragra* is a pretentious show of force carried out in a disagreeable way that does not often yield the desired result.

But making *gragra*, or this method of meeting force with an equal or greater opposite force may work well, as long as those under your sphere of influence are constrained and subordinate to your power pack. In the aforementioned example of teacher–student relationship, the students have no choice but to yield. Many unwise parents receive a rude awakening when they fail to notice that their wards have slowly crept into adulthood and their once effective methods from the past are now obsolete. Trying to use *gragra* on a Junior who now towers above you is no longer a good idea. Instead, gentle persuasion cloaked in reasoning is required.

There are no ties as natural and powerful as the parent-child relationship. You may choose friends or who to marry or the organization you belong to, but you cannot choose your parents. As close as this relationship may be, time comes when power must shift into one of mutual respect, where the yielding of rights and positions is purely voluntary for the common good.

As an adult, you might seek counsel and permission from your parents, out of respect and not out of necessity. Or your parents could reciprocate your respect by appointing you to deputize in a proceeding where they are active members. Meekness is having the power to remain on top but voluntarily remaining below, having the power to subdue or annihilate but refraining or resisting exertion of authority simply for the good of everyone involved.

When next you are faced with an aggressive situation, pause or apply the brakes and ask yourself what the deal is. If the deal is small, there is no need trying to haul the deal with excessive resources—you should reserve your *gragra* for the big one! If it is no deal or nothing spoils if you sheepishly walk away, then just walk away like the cleanest sheep in town. However, if you carefully determine that it is in fact a big deal, you may have to size up your resources to ensure you can successfully take on the challenge. Without ultimate power—which no human being has—it is impossible to take possession of something that belongs to everybody, if you are not in position or prepared to eliminate all opposition. It is foolhardy to try to use *gragra*, either covertly or overtly, to rob people of what rightfully belongs to them.

Once upon a time, you heard the story of a woman who used all the money she had saved for groceries to gamble. The card-playing young men took her money right in front of everybody, but there was nothing anyone could do because she fell for their cunning persuasion to make easy money. "Easy come, easy go," they say. If those young men had taken the money from this poor woman by gragra, you can bet there would have been some pants-tearing fracas and the crowd would not have been as forgiving.

Where there is an evil use of something

natural, look closely; there must be a good use for it, otherwise it would not be there. You have heard persuasive arguments where individuals flood their opponents and the public with reason after reason why their points are inline or superior, all made possible without resorting to brutal force, but only using words to convince the opposition. That is active persuasion, with the visible goal to win over your opponent.

On the other hand, if the deal is big enough to warrant involvement and you are not interested in taking the credit for coming up with the winning blow or formula, there is another option called passive persuasion. The required skills set and resources are the same, but you intentionally become passive to allow others hear what you have to say. The power of this method is displayed when your opponent disagrees with you on their own strong main point that you have already conceded to. During confrontation, most people behave like the puff adder, poised to strike but deaf to everything including what they are saying. "Sorry, I was so mad I could not think properly or hear what you were saying!" If you need this person's cooperation, the best course of action is to present the contribution in a passive format, so they can discover and absorb it through volition. This approach is useful because it pays to package your desired outcome in a neutral and sometimes inert state, with the intention that your opponents might uncover and activate your intent and even—if that is your wish—take the credit for bringing about the desired conclusion.

Without a doubt, this passive approach is not recommended for everyone. Since it has no attached immediate individual credit, it is useless and lackluster for those who only seek relevance.

So what is most important to you—who won the argument and who did what, or the fact that it is done well?

In the end, all that matters is that the goal was achieved.

Patience

The old school says, "The patient dog eats the fattest bone." But the new school asserts that in Nigeria, the patient dog is left with nothing to eat. If you are of the old school, you believe that there are enough bones for everyone, and what is for everyone belongs to everyone! No matter the size of the common pie, it must be shared, and the earlier you learn how to share it, the better off you are.

When a gate is narrow and there are many who must walk through, it only makes sense to file in one after the other in an orderly fashion. If collective patience is not exercised as the crowd approaches the narrow gate, the resulting bottleneck would prevent entry.

Imagine an accident on a highway, and the four-lane highway suddenly becomes one lane and everyone weaves through traffic to cram into that one lane still moving. If you operate impatiently—as your detractors expect you to—mayhem is inevitable.

Patience is like a brake mechanism that tells you when to stop, and what makes these brakes work are the protocols you carefully put in place ahead of time. Whenever the traffic lights of life's highway indicate yellow, those who are disciplined by way of training quickly recognize that it is time to get ready to apply the brakes. When it shows red, it means stop and you must hit your brakes as hard as you can or else you smash into head on collision and get killed or you kill another! This means that you have to know the power of your brakes.

But you must realize that patience is not the same as inaction. Patience includes orderly planning and putting in place structures that are considered fair and workable. Your turn arrives only after patiently waiting for others, but you must also be prepared to move on and make room for those who come after you.

This rule of engagement must be understood in order to maintain the line of succession, prohibiting the removal of the ladder of ascent that you abhor and are willing to protest in your birthday suit if necessary. Such notices of community norms are better presented and documented in a peaceful manner, rather than arbitrarily enforced without having been previously addressed or agreed to. At best, there should be a public warning amongst all stakeholders that things are no longer business as usual. Actions like removing ladders, closing gates, and acting as an unofficial gateman are unacceptable.

Fairness demands that people in front of the queue understand these expectations: knowing that the flow stops if you forget that the goodies are for everyone. If you are privileged to be on the inside, you have the mandate to open doors and even windows that have yet to be accessed by the people patiently waiting their turn. Any drastic measure that precludes the establishment of this rule of engagement is draconian and unbrotherly. People have always taken turns, but if there is a paradigm shift, all stakeholders must be warned about it.

You can learn the lesson of the Ogoni people without reliving its consequences: though you may not be personally capable of murder, your words and the positions you take can incense others to violence. In times of success, there is an ever-present temptation to hoard the spoils. But when managing failure, people are forced to band together to win. If you struggle together, it is only fair that you also eat together.

You need patience, trust, goodwill and resolve paired with a decent dose of aggression, but you must be fair to others. Those before you may have gotten away with the largesse that came with their positions, but the opportunities that you currently enjoy are due to the fact that countless others stepped aside to make room for you. Now, those behind you are patiently waiting for you to do the same for them. If you do not fight alone, it makes sense that you will never eat alone.

"The fly that does not know when the funeral is over goes to the grave with the corpse," says an Izon proverb.

A Word is enough for the wise.

Periodic Table of Friendship

Friends are priceless, no doubt about it. You have no choice of who becomes your blood relative, but you can choose your friends and they can choose you. Unlike your relatives, even after a friendship is established, your friend has to be pleased or have a cogent reason to retain you as a friend. The manner you keep and maintain something precious determines the ease with which you use it when required.

If you don't take care of your friendships, you are like those who store all their important documents in a file cabinet in a haphazard manner. When the need arises—and it will—to retrieve those documents, you would most likely feel frustrated because you can't find your important files and might be forced to use a less suitable item.

You need others to supplement and complement you in areas where you clearly need assistance. Some people are blessed with loads of family members who double as friends they can run to for assistance. Thankfully, those without siblings can acquire friends. But remember a person who wants friends must show themselves friendly, and the best friends are made, not bought.

Do you now see how there can be various categories of friendship? A few are your bosom friends, while some are your dependable friends, faithful and trusted friends, others your casual friends, your mutual friends, and acquired friends, but it doesn't stop there. The key is to know the kind of friend a particular individual is to you. For a friendship to hold, there should be a shared understanding of potential benefit to both parties. What either of you desire or expect from the association may not be the same, but there must be some understanding of mutual advantage.

For you who possess the gift of benevolence to exercise liberality, the recipient must be humble enough to receive the gift without strings attached. Without a receiver, there will be no giving. The key ingredient that maintains such friendship is the absence of guilt or suspicion of any exploitation. Since the motive behind friendships and the strings that sustain them are varied among friends, it is difficult to clearly claim that one class or type of friendship is somehow best compared to the others.

As such, the term "Best Friend" is a misleading misnomer because you can only measure best in instances where the yardsticks are the same. Friendship is a relationship. It would be odd to refer to one brother or sister as a best brother/sister. Hence, wouldn't other descriptive terms such as closest friend, bosom friend and most trusted friend be considered more appropriate?

All your life, you have heard well-meaning people say it is best to have a few close quality friends, but aren't you beginning to wonder if that is really the best idea?

The reason behind such noble statements is the assumption that many friends may cause distraction and potential conflicts of interest. Distraction is often the byproduct of disorderliness and the lack of knowing what you want or what you have. They say the dog is a man's best friend, but is man a dog's best friend?

Mutuality is different from equality, and every party in a friendship exists for a mutual benefit, which in most cases is different and unequal. So should it come as any surprise that you may not be the best friend of your best friend? A lack of understanding of this fundamental concept often leads to the breakups of otherwise useful friendships.

Friendship is a voluntary association of convenience that exists between two or more consenting human beings. For friends to thrive and be happy in the friendship, the parties must be ready and willing to treat one another as human beings. The mantra should be *use things and love people*, not the other way around. When a friend feels used or abused in the relationship, distrust takes root and lack of interest follows suit.

The next thing after differentiating people from things is to evaluate or assess the value of your friends. You must quickly know and be willing to let your friends know how much you value their friendship. The more specific you are in your affirmation, the better you are in your quest for maintaining friendships. Without meaning to compare humans with elements, friendships can be better managed if the value of the friends are assessed and mentally stored like in a Chemistry Periodic Table.

Friendship is a form of bonding, just as bonding between the elements of a periodic table. All bonds are not equal. There are bonds such as ionic bonding and covalent bonding where some bonds are best kept loose, while others are strong and permanent as Araldite.

The management of expectation is crucial to maintain a friendship. Expectations between friends are similar to the ionic makeup of elements which must be known and kept at the fingertips to ensure effective bonding. Lack of understanding or ignorance of this vital premise could be costly. Two long-time friends who have done well over the years can lose their friendship when a third individual with a different makeup or vibe is introduced into the relationship.

If you do not know the value or the content (which is different from worth), it is easy to clutter your mind like a disorganized closet, and this lack of order can result in you reaching out for the 'wrong' friend who isn't equipped to serve the purpose of your friendship.

In such a case, don't blame your friend because the fault lies with you for having the wrong expectation, rather than your friend being a wrong friend. The mental arrangement of friends is to help you know who to run to when a need arises. The friend with the listening ear may not necessarily be the one with the spiritual, financial or physical muscles. Having wrong expectations of the wrong friend is unwise and will cost you.

But how are you supposed to "classify" your friends so as not to fall into the trap of wrong expectations? To help in this crucial task of proper classification, some form of periodic table of friendship is required. Amongst friends, it is necessary to know why a particular individual is a friend and arrange who does what in the friendship. That way, you know who to approach in the time of your need and eliminate the scrooge of wrong expectations. By knowing the capabilities and the qualities of your friends, you stand a better chance of enjoying and maintaining your friendship. Isn't it incredibly stressful when your friend expects you to do something you don't feel capable of doing, or worse, something you would never do voluntarily?

If you keep an array of the qualities and the value of your friends, you help to eliminate the inadvertent misplacement of needs at the doorsteps of friends who are ill-equipped for the situation.

In chemistry terms, it is as if you are expecting a covalent bond where an ionic bond should be. Every human being has value and a purpose, and that is how God the Creator meant it to be. So live a purposeful life and be good to others and make as many friends as you are capable of maintaining, but remember that anyone in a friendship remains in that relationship for a reason. Part of being a good friend is to know the reason why the person calls you "friend" and aspire to give the best of what they need from you. And do not be shy at letting your friend know what attracts you to the friendship. Be courageous and liberal enough to affirm your friends on their conduct within the relationship.

A loyal friend is useful to everyone, so be that good friend to the good one. And if you are a good friend, you will eventually find the good one.

The musings of Akiroro have now ended, so now it is time for you to keep talking, until he starts talking again. Keep the faith.

Discussion Questions

Bending Corners

a. In what instance can self-disclosure be too much information? Why should timing be taken into consideration with full disclosure in relationships?
b. How can you avoid or lessen bending corners in your life?
c. Are there times when it is best to obscure your motive in order to get what you want?

As A Man Thinketh

a. Are there people or places you have labeled as "bad" solely based on what you have heard from others about them?
b. Name something that you once thought you would never do but now you do it often.
c. What type of media (i.e. TV, books) have you consumed in the past that influenced the way you think now?
d. What lies have you told so many

times that you now believe?

Autoimmunity

a. What idea have you held onto so long that it has created an image about yourself that is not necessarily true?
b. Do you base your value on the scars of your past? Why do you do so? Why is it so difficult to let go of those scars when your current self is far removed from your past self?
c. Was there ever a time when you thought that no one cared for you? Why did you think that? How do you feel about it now?

Befriending Your Neighbor

a. Do you treat other people the way you want to be treated?
b. How often do you reach out to people from other groups of life?

Communication is Not Mud Wrestling

a. Do you have friends or family you no longer talk to for reasons you can't quite remember?
b. How do you prefer to resolve

conflict? Is it better to deal with conflict head on or take a more diplomatic approach?

Corridors of Influence
a. What are the strongest relationships in your life? How have they influenced you and the people around you?
b. Are there people who have influenced you without knowing they did?
c. Are there people you can influence if you could only make more time?

Dreaded Bending Corners
a. Are you more likely to make peace or add fuel to an argument? Why?
b. Are there times when you should have spoken up to help someone but didn't? What made you not speak up? Would you be quiet again?
c. Was there ever a time when you thought that no one cared for you? Why did you think that? How do you feel about it now?

Granny's Three-Legged Pot
a. Do you impose tough restrictions on

your relationships? Do these restrictions make it hard for those relationships to function?
b. Do you accept your friends as they are, with their good and bad, or are you always trying to change people to be more like you?

How Many Enemies Do You Have?
a. Do you agree that you are your own worst enemy?
b. Does forgiveness come easy to you?
c. Is it practical to treat people better than they deserve or treat you?

Kaleidoscope in Humanity
a. What are your blind spots or faults that you never realized until someone told you about them? How did you react?
b. How rigid are you when it comes to going against your beliefs?
c. Are you open to understanding other's point-of-view or are you more concerned with making them see your picture of life?

Kiripoi
a. How often do you end up in

troublesome situations simply because you didn't take time to understand what is going on around you?
b. Have you ever found something important that you weren't looking for? What did you find?

Moving the Goal Post
a. In today's society, what norms or beliefs do you think are outdated? Why do you continue to observe these norms?
b. Do you think women are equal to men? If so, why do you think they are equal? If not, why do you think women are inferior or superior to men?

Ownership Is in the DNA
a. Is it the responsibility of all the adults in a society to raise the children and not just the parents of the children?
b. Has a breakdown in family structure and values led to a decay in society?

Passive Persuasion
a. Are you guilty of using *gragra* (pretentious show of force) on

people under your authority or on people who you know can't fairly resist you?
b. Do you think meekness or humility is overrated or underrated? Why?
c. Is getting credit for doing something more important than doing that thing well, regardless of who gets the credit?

Patience
a. Do you believe patience is a good virtue?
b. Do your words have consequences? What is more important to you: good character or good words?
c. Do you believe that you owe something to the people coming after you, to make room for them and help them succeed?

Periodic Table of Friendship
a. Does the proposed method of ranking or grouping types of friendship eliminate any spontaneity of making friends?
b. Do you think the "absence of guilt or suspicion of any exploitation" is the key ingredient of friendship?
c. In the chapter, there is a chance of "wrong expectations" when we do not classify our friends correctly. How would you approach a possibly awkward conversation of defining a friendship?
d. How do you manage shifting needs and/or seasons in friendships?

Glossary

Term	Meaning
Izon	A language spoken a majority of the Ijaw people of Nigeria.
Cabuluka	A mild antiseptic soap containing carbolic acid, and is used in a range of industrial and consumer applications. A skin irritant.
Gragra	The pretentious show of force or doing things in a rush or aggressively to get your way.
Krinn	A no-nonsense, forceful response to "gragra"
Ogoni	A tribe in Rivers State, Nigeria.
Ogirizi	An evergreen tree also known as Newbouldia laevis, native in Central and West Africa.

Tue: Joel 2:23, Isaiah 65:24, 66:8-9, Psalm 46,
Isaiah 43:18-19 Matthew 7:7
Wed: Exodus 14:14-18, Heb 11:11, 1 Samuel 1, 2 Samuel 9,
Matthew 19:1-6, Romans 8

361-896-7615

12/27/23
12/26/23, 12/28/23,
Rume (chioma): 346-946-1140

1219958139
Uncle Fred: 803-226-9308

14,965,545.92   1/17/24

Igho fees
1,720
 800
2,520 due for Feb 8, 2024
Fcmb
Oghenero: 882 180 9010